Swing Trading

Learn the Secrets to Increasing Your Monthly Income With Swing Trading

Ethan Boson

© Copyright 2020 by Ethan Boson. All right reserved. The work contained herein has been produced with the intent to provide relevant knowledge and information on the topic described in the title for entertainment purposes only. While the author has gone to every extent to furnish up to date and true information, no claims can be made as to its accuracy or validity as the author has made no claims to be an expert on this topic. Notwithstanding, the reader is asked to do their own research and consult any subject matter experts they deem necessary to ensure the quality and accuracy of the material presented herein.

This statement is legally binding as deemed by the Committee of Publishers Association and the American Bar Association for the territory of the United States. Other jurisdictions may apply their own legal statutes. Any reproduction, transmission or copying of this material contained in this work without the express written consent of the copyright holder shall be deemed as a copyright violation as per the current legislation in force on the date of publishing and subsequent time thereafter. All additional works derived from this material may be claimed by the holder of this copyright.

The data, depictions, events, descriptions and all other information forthwith are considered to be true, fair and accurate unless the work is expressly described as a work of fiction. Regardless of the nature of this work, the Publisher is exempt from any responsibility of actions taken by the reader in conjunction with this work. The Publisher acknowledges that the reader acts of their own accord and releases the author and Publisher of any responsibility for the observance of tips, advice, counsel, strategies and techniques that may be offered in this volume.

Table of Contents

Introduction 6
Chapter 1: What Is Swing Trading 9
  Figuring Out Swing Trading 9
  Swing Trading vs. Day Trading 11
  Trading Tactics 16
  Know Your Risk So You Can Trade Confidently 17
Chapter 2: Tools and Platforms 18
  Brokers That Offer Technical Analysis Tools 18
  Technical Analysis Sites 22
Chapter 3: Financial Instruments 28
  ETF 29
  Options 30
  Forex 32
  Cryptocurrencies 33
Chapter 4: Risk Management 36
  Position Size 37
  The One-Percent Rule 40
  Setting Take-Profit and Stop-Loss 40
  Market Environment 42
  Expected Return 43
  Hedge and Diversify 43
Chapter 5: Fundamental Analysis 45
  Earnings 47
  Intrinsic Value 49
  Criticisms of Fundamental Analysis 49
Chapter 6: Technical Analysis 51
  Limitations 52
  Analysis of Terminology 53
    Long 53
    Bullish 54

    Short *54*
    Bear *55*
   Bar Chart 56
   Candlestick Charts 58
Chapter 7: Guiding Principles **62**
   Capital Preservation 64
   Discipline 65
   Margin 65
   Creating a Trading Plan 66
Chapter 8: Rules **72**
   Penny Stocks 74
Chapter 9: Strategies **77**
   Ten and 20-Day SMA 77
   Channel Trading 78
   Resistance and Support Triggers 79
   Fibonacci Retracement 79
Chapter 10: Entry and Exit **81**
   Entry Strategy 81
   Exit Strategies 83
Chapter 11: Creating a Routine **88**
   Pre-Market 88
   Market Hours 91
   The Market After Hours 93
Conclusion **94**

Introduction

First off, I would like to thank you for choosing this book and hope you find the information helpful and informative. In this book, we will talk about the different aspects of swing trading and how to start a successful business for yourself.

There are many different types of trading out there. Swing trading is one of those strategies. Just like any other type of trading, it can be successful or not. That's why it's important that you know what you're doing and how to do it. That's what this book is here to do.

The first thing we will go over is what swing trading is. It is different than day trading, and it's important to know what you're getting into. The lifestyle of swing trading is very different than most trading professions.

Then we will move into discussing the tools and platforms needed for trading. Trading requires brokers and other software to trade successfully. They aren't all made the same, so you have to pick the one that will work for you.

After that, we will look at what you can trade. Everybody is aware of stocks. They are the most common traded item, but you can choose many other things from like options, ETFs, currencies, and cryptocurrencies. You will have to decide which one works best for your needs.

Next, we will look at risk management. This is probably the most important chapter because your risk management strategy can help you succeed or fail as a trader. It can either cost you everything or help you hold onto some money that you could have lost.

The next two chapters will look at different analysis tools. The first is fundamental and deals with the basic information of a stock like revenue and earnings per share. Then there is technical analysis, which is reading all of the charts about stocks. These can be difficult for some people to understand, but we'll try to make this part as easy to understand as possible.

Then, we will look at the guiding principles. This will help you to be successful at swing trading by helping you treat this process as a business and coming up with a plan. After that, we'll go over "rules." While there aren't hard and fast rules for swing trading, there is some basic information most people will choose to follow. This will also look at trading penny stocks and why you need to be careful if you choose to do so.

Next, we'll look at proven strategies that you can use for swing trading. These strategies can help you get started in trading, but you don't have to follow them if you find that they don't work for you.

After that, we'll look at entry and exit strategies. These are some of the most important strategies to have as they will dictate how much money you make or lose. Lastly, we'll go over creating a trading routine. A routine can help you make more money as you aren't guessing what you should do each day.

There are a lot of books about swing trading on the market, so thank you for choosing this one. If you find any part of it helpful, please leave a review.

Chapter 1: What Is Swing Trading

Swing trading is a type of trading that tries to get gains that are either short or medium in any type of stock or another financial tool that happens within a couple of days or several weeks. Swing traders normally used some kind of technical analysis to help them find trading opportunities. These kinds of traders might use fundamental analysis along with looking at patterns and price trends.

Figuring Out Swing Trading

Normally, swing trading will involve holding either a short or long position for multiple sessions but not any longer than a few weeks or months. Keep in mind that this is just a normal time frame since some trades could last longer than a few months, but you can still think of them as swing trades. You can also do swing trading during any trading session, even though this is extremely rare. This kind of trading happens due to very volatile conditions.

The main goal behind swing trading is to grab a chunk of potential money. Some traders will try to find volatile stocks that are moving a lot while others like stocks that are more sedate. It really doesn't matter what the case might be; swing trading is a process where you have to figure out where a potential stock's price will move to next, get into a position, and then grabbing a chunk of money if that particular move actually happens.

Successful swing traders only want to grab onto that expected money and then find the next opportunity. Swing trading is among the most popular types of trading where they look for opportunities by using various types of technical analysis. If you are seriously interested in swing trading, you need to be very familiar with technical analysis.

Most swing traders will find trades on a reward or risk basis. If you analyze an asset's chart, it can help you figure out where the stock will enter, place a "stop loss," and then figure out where you can get out and make a profit. If you are risking only one dollar per share on a stock that could produce a three dollar gain, this is a very favorable reward to risk ratio. But if you risk one dollar only to make one dollar or 75 cents, this isn't as favorable.

Swing traders only use technical analysis because of the shorter time limits on the trades. With that being said, you can also use fundamental analysis to enhance your analysis. Look at this example: if you notice a bullish setup with one stock, you might want to see that the asset's fundamentals look good and are improving.

Swing traders will usually try to find stocks on daily charts, and they might watch either 15-minute or one-hour charts to find where they should enter, stop loss, and the level where they can make a profit.

To make it a bit simpler, here is a list of pros and cons to help you:

Pros
- Traders can rely on technical analysis to help make the process simple.
- It maximizes your profits by grabbing most of the market swings.
- Doesn't take as much time to make a trade as it does with day trading.

Cons
- Traders can sometimes miss longer trends for shorter market moves.
- Sudden reversals could result in huge losses.
- The trade positions could be subject to weekend and overnight risks within the market.

Swing Trading vs. Day Trading

Most active traders will put themselves into one of two groups: swing traders and day traders. Both want to see profits from moving stocks, but which one is better. The biggest difference between day trading and swing trading is normally their holding time. Swing trading usually involves an overnight hold normally, but day traders will close out their position before the close of the market on any given day. To break it down further, day trading gets limited to only one day, while swing trading might involve holding onto the stock for days or weeks.

When you hold onto a stock overnight, you might incur all the unpredictability that can happen, like gaps that could go either down or up against the stock's position. When you take an overnight risk, you are normally done with a smaller size than day trading, assuming that two different traders have accounts that are about the same size. Day traders usually use larger position sizes and might use a margin of 25 percent.

Swing traders have access to leverage or a margin of 50 percent. This basically means that if you are approved for margin trading, you will only need to have $25,000 in the capital for any trade that has a value of $50,000.

Swing Trading
This has to do with finding the swings within commodities, currencies, and stocks that happen for several days. Swing traders may go on for a couple of days and upwards of a few weeks to get them to work out. Swing traders are normally not full-time traders, although they could decide to transition to day trading and still swing trade every now and then.

Anybody who has some knowledge and capital could try their hand at swing trading. Due to the longer time-frame, swing traders don't have to be glued to their computers all day. They could work a full-time job along with swing trading.

- You can do swing trading with a single computer and all of the normal tools. It doesn't require any fancy technology.
- Because swing trading isn't usually a full-time job, there isn't a large chance of getting burned out because of the high-stress levels. Swing traders normally have normal jobs or other sources of income that they can use to offset their trading losses.
- Swing trading could result in some large losses since you are holding onto positions for a lot longer than day traders. This means that you have to face the risk of bigger losses.
- Swing traders could set some stop losses. Even though you have a chance of a stop being triggered when the stock reaches a price you don't like, it beats all of the constant monitoring you would have to do with your open positions when day trading.
- Because swing trading normally involves positions that are held overnight, the margin requirements will be higher. The maximum leverage is normally double your capital. This could be compared to day trading, where you have margins that come out to be four times a person's capital.
- Trades need some time to work themselves out. Keeping trades open for a couple of days or weeks might give you larger profits than day trading the same security several times throughout the day.

Day Trading
This is just what the name says it is. It involves making many trades in one day. This gets based on sophisticated charting and technical analysis. A day trader's main objective is making lots of money from trading commodities, currencies, or stocks through tiny amounts of profits throughout several trades. At the same time, they cap their losses on trades that don't bring a profit. Day traders don't normally keep any securities or positions overnight.

The largest lure to day trading is the possibility of getting huge profits. This will only happen for people who have the needed traits like diligence, discipline, and decisiveness required to be a successful day trader.

The US SEC says that "day traders normally suffer some financial losses during their first months of trading. Some of them never graduate to the status of making money." While the SEC will warn day traders that they should only risk that money they can afford to lose, the reality of day traders is that they create a lot of losses on money that has either been borrowed from friends or from margined trades. Those losses might not stop their career of day trading but could put them into a sizeable debt.

- For most finance jobs, having the right degree is a prerequisite just to get an interview. Day trading doesn't require an education. Even though there aren't any educational

requirements, taking some classes about computerized trading and technical analysis might help.
- Day trading can be stressful since you have to watch multiple screens for trading opportunities and then act fast to exploit them. You have to do this all day long, every day. You have to have a huge degree of concentration and focus. This could lead to burnout.
- In order to make a go at it, day traders will have to quit their job and the security of having a regular paycheck. From that day forward, they have to depend completely on their efforts and skills to create the money that they need to pay their bills and still live a great life.
- Day traders who have been at it for a long time love pitting their wits against other professionals and the market every day. This adrenaline rush is something that most traders won't admit to. But it tends to be a big reason why they make some of the decisions that they make as a day trader. They are going to be content spending their day poring over numbers in a cubicle.
- Day traders will have to compete with all of the other professionals, high-frequency traders, and hedge funds who can afford to spend millions of dollars in order to have an advantage. With this type of job, day traders don't have any choice but to spend a lot of money on the best computers, charting software, and trading platforms. Other

expenses might include costs for getting live quotes and commissions that could add up due to how many trades you do.
- A day trader will work alone. They are independent of all the corporate "bigwigs." They can have a flexible schedule, work at their own pace, and take time off anytime they want to. This is totally different than a person who is on a corporate treadmill.

Trading Tactics

Swing traders like to look for patterns on multiple day's charts. The most common patterns involve moving triangles, flags, "head and shoulders patterns," "cup-and-handle patterns," and "moving average crossovers. Candlesticks that show key reversals might be used with other indicators to create a solid trading plan.

Basically, every swing trader has to create a strategy and plan that will give them a better edge overtrades. This might involve looking for setups that will lead to more predictable movements with the stock's price. This is not easy, and there isn't one set up or strategy that will work every single time. With a favorable reward to risk ratio, you don't have to win each time. The more favorable the reward to risk ratio is, then you won't have to win as many times to create a profit with various trades.

Know Your Risk So You Can Trade Confidently

If you would like to make some exciting and fast trades, you will have to know how to manage your risk. With some indexes, you will know your maximum loss or profit before you ever trade. This means that you can make decisions with confidence. You have the ability to trade 23 hours each day, six days every week, and this included overnight and during lunch. It is trustworthy and transparent trading, where you won't ever lose any more than you put into it. You can trade all you want from one platform without incurring any broker fees or having to go through a broker.

Chapter 2: Tools and Platforms

The most important part in order to be a successful trader is able to look at the patterns within the trading data. Some technical analysis techniques can take all the emotion out of your trading decisions. Technical analysis systems could generate selling and buying indicators. It can also help you spot other opportunities with the number of improvements that have happened to these tools and how fast it can access millions of data points over the last 15 years. Anybody who trades online has access to these tools.

Some of the bigger trading sites will provide you with analysis tools to help out the new traders understand all of the main concepts. Most of these resources will be free to use, or they will be included with your broker account. However, there are some who might charge you. We will be looking at some of the analysis tools included in what a broker offers you and some other resources. These are listed randomly and are in no way ranking these in any order.

Brokers That Offer Technical Analysis Tools

The majority of the brokers we'll be talking about will use Recognia, which is a third-party system. Recognia is a Canadian company with great analysis tools that most brokers have worked on their trader platforms. These tools will automatically analyze how the price is moving so that it can find and understand chart patterns and any other condition based on the other practices within the analysis. The notifications will provide you with insight into the weaknesses and strengths of the stocks you are thinking about. These tools can't be accessed by investors who aren't a part of a brokerage platform. You should see their technology within their site.

Tradier

This is a very interesting beat. They offer market data, trading engine, and management systems to brokerage accounts. Market data and account settings are found in the cloud to give the customers the chance to log in to their accounts and trade from any partner. When you use the API, any designer can launch their own algorithmic system for trades, mobile apps, or trading platforms for customers. Being able to bring in a third-party tool to an account isn't something new, but some brokers will be able to do it. Tradier was the first to make this a central point of the business model.

TradeStation

Statistical modeling and technical analysis of trading strategies is the strength behind this platform. This company grew from a technical analysis software firm called "Omega Research." They have a downloadable platform that gives them the ability to make charts based on tick data. An automatic analysis has been built into this, and it provides you with patterns on charts as soon as they are created. Their web charting capabilities include toolbars that have access to styles, sessions, drawing tools, and time frames. This is the best application available from any broker. Any user can backtest and create a system that is based on technical occurrences. TradeStation comes with all of the tools you need. It has a huge historical database that lets you backtest your strategies.

Thinkorswim
This is TD Ameritrade's advanced platform lets traders customize their own platform with their trade ticket and favorite tools. Even though this platform was created for options trading, you can also find plenty of analytical tools that a swing trader can use. They have drawing tools, data visualization tools, and technical indicators. It also provides traders with the chance to create their own tools along with using Thinkorswim's built-in language. Its desktop version is very powerful, but you can use their mobile app or web version. All of these include streaming real-time data that can power over 400 technical studies.

Lightspeed
This was created for frequent traders. It has a customizable market scanner that will help you to find the best opportunities for trades. It will look through the whole stock universe so that it can show you symbols that have been filtered and sorted based on your requirements. It has over 100 criteria that can be used to search for things and combined them. It has a lot of customized charting tools and more than 20 years of trading data. There is a demonstration version that is available for people who want to take a test drive.

Interactive Brokers
All of the interactive brokers' platforms are very customizable, and it includes real-time streaming and hundreds of indicators. It contains technical analysis tools that are very advanced with more than 30 years worth of trading data and 120 indicators. They also have a demonstration version that gives you the chance to figure out how to work the platform. It also lets you test some trading scenarios. You can also attach a third-party analytical platform to your account.

Fidelity Investments
Fidelity has a downloadable trading interface called Active Trader Pro. It offers a deeper set that is available on their website. It gives you customizable trade tools and charting functions immediately. Its software alerts you to any technical signals in any stock that you follow. It also gives you alerts to any open positions. Its web-based charting uses events and technical patterns that are given through Recognia. This advanced charting gives you the ability to see more than 60 customizable indicators, extended hours of data, 30 days of days, and 40 years of price data.

E*Trade
The active platform of this is On Power. This is a live-action scanner that contains over 100 screens that can scan through the market for live analytical metrics and prices that have been based on news, sentiment, earnings, fundamental, and technical events. It can uncover oversold and overbought stocks that help you

look through more opportunities in your portfolio. The majority of the screens they have are unique to them. Its scanner allows you to look through stocks based on events and patterns. It will send you alerts when any new criteria get met.

Charles Schwab
This platform uses real-time data that allows its clients to filter through ETFs and stocks based on fundamental and technical requirements. Traders are able to set certain parameters that they find important and then use the results within their watch lists. They also have customizable charts that use Recognia's tools that can recognize patterns. Using mobile devices gives you some technical analysis indicators even though there aren't any drawing tools.

Technical Analysis Sites
eSignal
This is the most esteemed name within the technical analysis world. It was launched back in the mid-1990s. You can download it on any Windows-based software package that offers data from global exchanges, customizable charting, backtesting of strategies, and technical studies. By using API, you can trade with several brokers at once, including Interactive Brokers and Tradier. It is a bit pricey. The basic version uses data that is delayed by 15 minutes, and it only offers you 25 studies. It will cost you $54 per month. The signature version that runs on data in real-time gives you hundreds of studies and will cost

you $176 per month. They do offer you a ten percent discount if you pay for an entire year at one time.

TrendSpider
This was created in 2016, and it has a huge array of tools that have been created to help you plan, time, and find the trades you want to make with better precision and efficiency. You will be able to generate a dynamic watch list by using a Market Scanner that can look through timeframes that can be one minute out to one month. They already have a lot of scanners built it, or you have the option of designing your own. You will have access to real-time data and more than 20 years of trading information without any more money. This is a web-based platform, and any customizations you create will be stored in the cloud. They have a charting package that gives you a chance to back-test all the strategies you come up with. They have subscriptions that start at $33 and go up to $97 per month. They do offer discounts for plans that you prepay a year in advance.

TradingView
This has more than 100 indicators that have been combined with lots of other tools that will cover cryptocurrencies, global stocks, and currencies. It uses the Pine Script language, which gives you the chance to change existing indicators or develop something from scratch. Their public script library provides you with access to thousands of scripts that other members have published. You can use only a limited number of them for free. A subscription will give access to more data and features. This can run you

anywhere from $14.95 to $59.95 each month. They do have a paper trading system built-in, or you can choose to link up another broker account like TradeStation.

TradeIdeas

This company was created in 2004 and works with market professionals, traders, and subscriber investors in more than 65 countries. Its system has 243 filters and 311 alerts that include social media, technical, fundamental, and other data sets. It can also identify swing trading and short-term opportunities. Subscribers could create formulas by themselves, and they could build custom watch lists along with real-time alerts. You can backtest and trade on the systems within their simulated environment. Those who have a premium subscription that has connected accounts can perform live trades using the TradeIdeas platform. This platform links with other charting and trading platforms. This can be downloaded to any Windows platform and has a web version that allows you to access it on any device. Their basic subscription is $118 per month or $1068 a year. Their premium service will run you $228 per month or $2268 a year.

TickerTocker

This was created in 2018 and offers its users several trading services that include automated trading resources, research, and education. You have the ability to follow other members who have been given the title of Leader or just use their creation tools to come up with your own tools. These strategies can be backtested with their historical data to see if it will perform well. Their charting system that is built-in will give you the chance to overlay price charts with their technical indicators. This platform is compatible with several brokers like TradeStation, Fidelity Investments, Tradier, TD Ameritrade, and E*Trade. You are able to join and use most of their features free even though they charge for some of their premium services.

StockCharts
This lets you create yearly, quarterly, monthly, weekly, daily, and "intraday price charts," "seasonality charts," "yearly price charts," "relative rotation graphs," "point and figure charts," and a lot more. There are more than 1000 technical indexes and indicators along with real-time data for several cryptocurrencies like Bitcoin Cash, Litecoin, XRP, Ethereum, and Bitcoin. This means you can perform technical analysis with cryptocurrencies, which is unique for them. You are able to use some features for free, but monthly subscriptions give you more studies and more data. This can range anywhere between $14.95 and $39.95.

Slope of Hope
The slope of Hope got its start in 2005 when Tim Knight sold Prophet.net to TD Ameritrade so he could share the things he had learned with friends. This is now the place to go for discussions, charts, trading ideas, technical analysis with all kinds of traders. Most of these features are free, and they rival the capabilities of the expensive sites. Its main feature is its rules that allow you to come up with test trading

systems. All you have to do is drag and drop the rules that you would like your charts to have then tested them out. Then you will be able to set up alerts to tell you when your conditions have been met.

NinjaTrader

This gives you a trading environment that allows you to simulate, build, and test a system for forex, futures, and equities before you start investing any real money into the market. You can use their backtesting, trade simulation, and charting tools for free, but you will be charged some fees for certain indicators that are created by third-party developers. You can find more than 100 technical indicators within the basic package along with research tools, trade journaling, charting, and fundamentals. Through API, you can add NinjaTrader to TD Ameritrade, FXCM, OANDA, and Interactive Brokers, or you could just use NinjaTrader's brokerage services.

MetaStock

This player has been around for quite some time, too. It was created back in the late 1980s. There are a lot of different versions out there. The most commonly used one is MetaStock R/T. It uses real-time data from whichever exchange you want to use. It also has more than 150 line studies and indicators that could help you learn how to trade on each indicator. If you are an experienced user, it allows you to write your indicators. You could build some trading strategies by yourself or work through the included strategies. This can identify over 30 candle patterns on charts and give you advice on ways to use them. This subscription will cost you about $100 per month, with data feeds costing extra. It connects through API to other online brokers.

Chapter 3: Financial Instruments

In order to be a trader, you are going to have to have something to trade. While the most common thing to trade is stocks, there are quite a few other options to pick from. Seeing as stocks are the most common, let's take a look at what stocks are.

Simply put, stocks are shares of a company. When you purchase a stock, you are buying an ownership share in that company. Something most people don't realize is that, while you can sit next to Tim Cook at Apple's shareholder meeting, you do have a right to vote at the meetings, if you so choose to do so. But the main reason a person will invest in a stock is to earn a return. The price of a stock appreciates, which means you can sell it and earn a profit. There are stocks that also pay dividends, but as a swing trader, you won't be holding onto a stock long enough to earn a dividend.

For long-term stockholders, the average annual return is ten percent, which goes down to seven to eight people after inflation. That means if you had, 30 years ago, invested $1,000 in stocks, they would be worth over $8,000 today.

As a swing trader, it's important to research the company before you choose to invest in a stock. You won't be keeping it for more than maybe a week, but you want to make sure that there is a good chance that it will appreciate in value during that time. When you do invest in a stock, you won't be buying it directly from the company. Instead, you will likely be buying it from another trader. Just like you will be selling those same stocks to another trader.

All of these trades will take place in a stock exchange, with a broker working for the investor. A lot of people use online stockbrokers and will buy and sell through the broker's trading platform. You have to have an account in order to buy and sell stocks. Of the different things you can trade, stocks tend to be on the more volatile side because they are shares in a company. They depend on how well the stock market is doing, so during a recession or any type of economic turmoil, you are going to see that stocks trend down instead of up. That's why it could be a good idea to invest in more than just stocks, or you may want to stay away from stocks altogether.

ETF

ETF stands for the exchange-traded fund and is a security type that involves collecting securities that track an index. ETFs are similar to mutual funds. However, you will find them on exchanges, and ETFs can be trading throughout the day like stocks. A popular ETF is the SPDR S&P 500 ETF and tracks the S&P 500 index.

An ETF is like a file of several different types of securities, which can include commodities, bonds, stocks, or a mixture of all of them. It is marketable security, which means it has a price associated with it that allows it to bought and sold. ETFs can be bought and sold on the same exchanges like stocks. This is what sets them apart from mutual funds, and they are more liquid and cost-effective.

They operate a lot like stocks, but instead of buying a stock in one company, you will be buying a group of different assets. This is great for people who look for diversification. A single ETF can hold up to hundreds or even thousands of stocks throughout many different industries, or it could belong all to a single sector or industry. There are also different types of ETFs, including bonds, industry, commodity, currency, and inverse.

ETFs offer a lower average cost than what it would cost to buy each individual stock. You only have to execute one transaction to purchase and one to sell, which means fewer commissions since only a couple of trades are being done.

Options

Options are considered financial derivatives, which means they derive their value from an underlying stock or security. Options provide a buyer the right, but not the obligation, to buy or sell the stock at a certain price. Trading stocks could be looked at like gambling in a casino. You basically bet against the house, so you could win if you an incredible string of luck.

Options, on the other hand, is like betting on a horse race. Each person bets against another person. The track just takes a small cut. This makes it a zero-sum game. The gain of an option buyer is also the loss of the seller, and vice versa.

The main difference between stocks and options is that with a stock you own part of a company, while options are contracts that give you the right to get a stock at a certain price on a certain day.

There are two types of options, calls and puts. A call option means you have the right, but not the obligation, to buy the stock any time before the option expires. With a put option, you will have the right to sell, but you aren't obligated to.

Options are often held by the long-term investor to help offset their stock holdings during times that are volatile, but the swing trader who buys and sells options are after outsized profits. Their cost are cheap, and their returns can be way better than the underlying stock.

Swing trading options gives you the chance to take advantage of short-term stock shocks, no matter the range or depth. It's common to see some options triple or quadruple up overnight during the more explosive trading sessions.

Options trading can be tricky because you have to make sure you pick the right one at the right time, and figure out which direction you think the stock is going to go. If you believe that at stock is getting ready to reach a heavy short-term decline, then going with a put option with a close expiration to the current day would be a smart choice. If you believe a short-term decline is eventual, a call option several weeks or months out would be best.

Forex

Forex got its name from foreign currency and exchange. When you trade forex, then you are trading currencies, and buy and large, this is less volatile than stocks. This type of trading is the process of changing one currency into another. A lot of people believe that the best way to trade currencies is through swing trading.

Unlike the stock market, which can be traced back hundreds of years, the forex market as we know is still fairly new. Of course, if you look at it in its most basic sense, of people change one currency to a different one, forex has been around since nations started to mint currencies. Our modern markets was created in 1971 at Bretton Woods.

The act of trading currencies was very hard before the start of the internet. Most currency traders were hedge funds, high-net-worth individuals, or multinational corporations because forex required a lot of capital. Through the internet, a retail market came into being, and provided access to the foreign exchange markets.

While forex is often seen as safer than stocks, it can be complex and risky. The interbank market has different amounts of regulation, and their instruments aren't standardized. There are some areas of the world where it is completely unregulated. Banks have to determine and accept credit risk and sovereign risk, and they have come up with internal process to keep themselves safe.

Since the market is filled with banks providing bids and offers for certain currencies, the pricing mechanism is all about supply and demand. Since there are large trade flows, one rogue trader would find it hard to influence the price.

The perk of trading forex is that the markets are the largest when it comes to daily trading volume and offer more liquidity. This means it is easier to enter and exit a position.

Cryptocurrencies

The cryptocurrency is still a very new thing. It is a digital cash that gives a person the chance to send value through a digital setting. It is an electronic cash system that isn't owned by any one person. Cryptocurrencies are decentralized. The most common cryptocurrency is Bitcoin. These types of currencies are supposed to be safer than backs because of their blockchain. Investing in cryptocurrenices isn't a good idea for people who don't understand cryptocurrencies. If you understand them, and how they work, then by all means, trade them. Otherwise, you should learn about them before investing.

A lot of markets have times when they are closed, however, cryptos never close. It is a 24/7 market and you can access it seven days week, 365 days a year. This is why people should not day trade cryptos, and if you want to trade them, should us a swing trading strategy.

The biggest concern about trading and purchasing crytocurrencies is security and safety. That's why you want to make sure you pick a reliable exchange. Once you have picked a reliable exchange, the actual trading will become easier.

The best overall exchange for cryptos is Coinbase. It was founded in 2012, not long after the release of Bitcoin, and is licensed and regulated. It currently has licenses to operate in over 40 states and territories. It has a variety of altcoin choices, a simple user interface, and very liquid. Unfortunately, if you don't use the pro version, you will likely face high fees. You could see fees of $0.99 to $2.99 depending on how much your purchase is. I would suggest everybody starts with Coinbase.

However, if you are more advance in the cryptocurrency world, you could try Binance. It was founded in 2017, and is very big in altcoin trading. It offers nearly 600 different trading pairs. It has lower fees than other exchanges and advanced charting.

Unfortunately, there are 13 states who don't support Binance.

To make sure you pick the best exchange, you have to understand the different types. First there is a centralized exchange. Coinbase and Binance, along with Gemini and Kraken, are centralized. They are private companies that provide a platform to trade cryptocurrencies. They will require you to register and identify yourself.

They all have active trading, liquidity, and high volumes. That said, centralized exchanges aren't really in line with the Bitcoin philosophy. If the companies servers were to be compromised, the entire system might shut down. Worse, the users sensitive data could get out.

The second type is a decentralized exchange. They work like bitcoin. It does not have a central point of control. It's like a server, except each computer in the serve is spread all over the world, and each computer that makes up a part of it is controlled by a person. If one of those computers were to turn off, it doesn't affect the network because there are other computers that continue to run the network

Attacking something like that is a lot harder than a centralized network. These exchanges are not subject to rules of a regulatory body. People come and go, and that means you don't have to declare your identity and are free to use it in any manner they choose, legal or not.

Chapter 4: Risk Management

Risk management is used to help cut down your losses. It is what can prevent a trader from losing everything they have. Risk happens when you suffer a loss. If you can manage this, you can open yourself up to making more money. This is an often overlooked prerequisite to being a successful trader. You may be able to generate a lot of profits, but you can also lose it all with a couple of bad trades without having a risk management strategy. Let's look at how to come up with a successful risk management strategy.

First, you need to make sure that your broker is good for frequent trading. There are some brokers who cater to customers who trade infrequently. They have high commission rates and don't provide the analytical tools active traders need.

Take-profit and stop-loss points are two ways a trader can plan ahead. The successful trader will know the price that they are okay paying and what price they are willing to sell. These will all be measured against the odds of the stock reaching the goals that they have set. If their return is going to be high enough, then they will execute their trade.

On the other hand, the unsuccessful trader will enter a trade without knowing these points. Like gamblers, their emotions will start to overtake them and it will dictate how they act. Losses make a person want to hold on, hoping that they are going to win back their money, while profits can make them hold hoping for more gains.

Before we get into specific strategies, let's look at some questions that can help you manage risks. Before you make a trade, ask yourself these questions and ensure that you don't cut corners.

1. Is the security liquid?
2. Is it a penny stock?
3. Are you prepared for limiting your losses at the individual stock level?
4. Do you have a diversified portfolio?
5. Have you limited your total portfolio losses to seven percent?

Position Size

Position size is likely something that the new trader often doesn't think about. The proper position size is going to vary between traders, and will all depend on your account size. While there is a max size a new trader should use to make sure they don't experience a catastrophic failure, there is also a minimum size that can lead to a similar demise. If you are new to trading with a small account, then this is very important.

What's too small? A common question of first time traders is how much money will I need to start out? Unfortunately, there isn't an easy answer and the amount of capital you need will be different based on your trade plans. The first step to figure this out is to establish an understanding of what it will cost to make your trade. This needs to include the commissions that your broker charges and any fees that could be applied. Once you know how much it will cost to make a trade, you can look at the risk and reward to figure out how much capital you will need.

It may seem silly at first to think there is a position that is too small. It is not uncommon for the new trader to make the correct pick, sell a stock higher than it was bought, and still end up losing money. It is not free to trade, and your price per trade can vary depending on the broker. Fidelity charges $7.95 for each trade. Let's assume you are starting out with just $500. While it isn't impossible to grow that account, you have to think about the fact that you will be at a serious disadvantage and have a near zero chance of success. With a small account, discipline and rules are a lot more important.

For example, you are watching the (fake) symbol of EST and you start to like the price action. Its current price is $2.50 per share. You plan on starting small, so you use only $100 of your $500. You can buy 40 shares. A few days later the stock goes up $0.30 per share and you decide to sell. With the increase and your 40 shares, you make $112 or 12% return. That 12% is very acceptable and above average. Once the money has cleared the broker, you see that your account value has dropped by $4. You start trying to figure out why you lost that money on a winning trade and spot that horrible commission fee from your broker.

With this scenario, you are using the $7.95 cost. Your broker charges that each time you purchase shares and each time you sell. The trade netter you a $12 return, but the commission fees associated with the trade cost you $16, which leaves you with a loss of $4. Most new traders that have a small account will get wiped out by commission fees.

That means, there is not one single answer to how much money you need to start trading. The cost of trading will vary based on account size, stock price, risk tolerance, targer price, stop-loss, and is going to change with every trade. With the cost to trade in mind, you can start to figure out what your position should be. You need to make sure you have a large enough position to cover your commissions when you hit your target and that it is small enough that you don't risk more than two percent of your capital if you hit a stop-loss. A single winning trade can make up for a lot of losing trades, but only if you are using the right risk management strategy.

A lot of traders think they can figure out the position size by taking the difference of the entry price from a given stop-loss and use that to figure out the risk per share. This is a good starting point, but inefficient. The stop-loss needs to be placed at the point the invalidates the trade. In an ideal world, this would be the exact spot you will get out of your trade if it goes bad. Unfortunately, that is very rarely how it happens.

So coming up with a position size based on a stop-loss isn't enough.

The One-Percent Rule

Day traders will commonly follow this rule, but it's a good idea for swing traders to as well. Basically, this suggest that you shouldn't put more than one percent of your capital into one trade. That means if you have $20,000 in your account, your position should never be greater than $200.

This is normal for anybody who has less than $100,000 in their trading account. Some may choose to take things up to two percent, if they know for certain they can afford to do so. Those who have a higher balance may go with a lower percentage. This is because as the money in your account goes up, so does your position. The best way to make sure you keep your losses down is to make sure you stay under two percent. Any more than that and you could be risking a huge loss.

Setting Take-Profit and Stop-Loss

Stop-loss points is where you will sell and take a loss. This will happen when a trade doesn't go the way you had hoped. These points prevent you from thinking "it will come back" and puts a stop to the loss before it grows too big. For example, if it were to break below a key support level, traders will often sell as soon as they can.

The take-profit is the price where you will sell and take a profit. This occurs when additional upside is very limited due to the risks. For example, if you have a stock approaching a key resistance after a large move up, traders might want to sell before consolidation happens.

People normally figure out these points by performing a technical analysis, but it is also help to look at the fundamental analysis. For example, if you are looking at a stock ahead of earnings as the excitement builds, you may decide to sell before that news is released if the expectations have grown too much, no matter if your take-profit was reached.

Moving averages let you know where your might want to place the points as they are tracked throughout the market. Popular moving averages include five-, nine-, 20-, 50-, 100-, and 200-day averages. It is best to set these by applying them to the stock's chart and figuring out if the stock price has reacted to them previously as either a resistance or support level.

Another option for figuring out where to place these points is to use the trends lines for resistance and support. You can draw these out by connecting the past lows and highs that happened when there was significant volume. Much like when you look at the moving averages, it is important figure out levels where the price will react to the volume and trends. Once you have figured out these points, you will need to take these things into considerations:

- Look at the fundamental events, like earnings, as important periods to either enter or exit a trade as uncertainty and volatility changes.
- Adjust your stop-loss based on the volatility of the market. If there isn't a lot of change in the price, then you can tightened the stop-loss points.
- You don't need to place the stop-loss order any closer than 1.5X the current high-to-low range, as it may get executed for no reason.
- Adjust the moving averages so that they are matched to the target price. For example, you will need larger moving averages for longer targets to lower the signals
- Longer-term moving averages need to be used for volatile stocks to lower the odds that an unimportant price swing triggers an order.

Market Environment

It's important that you keep an eye on the health of the market environment to make sure that you have the right context and make more informed trade decisions. A good tool to do this is the Market Health Dashboard. It will measure two factors, trend and momentum. This will look at two different timeframes across three major averages, SPY QQQ and IWM.

This is then added into breadth cycles, which looks at different internal indicators and gives you an easy to read a bearish, bullish, or choppy score.

Expected Return

Setting these points is also an important part of coming up with your expected return. I cannot stress this enough, as this will force traders to think every trade through and make sure that they are rational. It will also provide you with a systematic way to compare your options for a trade and then pick the one that will help make you the most money. You can figure out this calculation with this formula:

"[(probability of gain) x (take profit % gain)] = [(probability of loss) x (stop-loss % loss)]"

What you get with this is an expected return, and then it will be measured against other opportunities to help you figure out which one of the stocks they should trade. You can calculate the probability of gain or loss through historical breakouts and breakdowns from resistance or support levels.

Hedge and Diversify

When it comes to trading, you should never put all of your eggs in one basket. If you do end up putting all of your money into a single stock or one instrument, you are only setting yourself up to make a big loss. That means you have to diversify the investments you make across both industry, market, and geographic region. This will not only lower your chance of risk, but it will show you many other opportunities that you may have otherwise missed.

You need to also spot the best time to hedge a position. Think about a stock position when the results are supposed to come in. You could think about taking the opposite through options, which will help to protect the position you took. Once all of the trading activity dies down, you can undo your hedge.

Chapter 5: Fundamental Analysis

Fundamental analysis is a way to measure the intrinsic value of a security by looking at related financial and economic factors. These analysts will look at whatever may affect the value of a stock. These factors could be macroeconomic factors, like the economy, or they could be microeconomic factors, such as how effectively the company is managed.

The overall goal of this is to find a number that a trader can use to compare it with the stock's price so that they can figure out if the stock is undervalued. This is thought to be the opposite of technical analysis, which looks to predict what direction a price may go through the analysis of historical information.

Any type of analysis performed on a stock is trying to figure out if the stock is correctly valued. Fundamental analysis is normally performed from the biggest information to the smallest to spot the securities that don't have the right price. Analysts will usually study, in a specific order, such as starting with the economy and then looking at the industry before they move into look at the specifics of the company.

For stocks, the fundamental analysis uses profit margins, return on equity, future growth, earnings, revenues, and other data to figure out the company's underlying value and potential for growth. You can find all of that information in the company's financial statement.

An analyst will come up with a model for figuring out the estimated value of a stock based on the public data. This is only an estimate of what a company should have the stock priced at. This is sometimes called the intrinsic value.

If you find that an analyst says that the value of a stock should be higher than what it is, they might publish a buy or overweight rating. This is a recommendation. If they find that there is a lower intrinsic value, then the stock should be seen as overvalued, and they will recommend that you sell.

People who follow these recommendations will expect that it will be safe to purchase a stock with a favorable rating because there is a better chance the price will go up later. Likewise, if the stock has been given a bad rating, then the price is expected to fall. These are all stocks that should probably be removed from portfolios and moved into "short positions."

Whether you plan on doing an in-depth analysis yourself, it's a good idea to understand the key ratios and terms so that you will find it easier to follow the stocks more accurately.

Earnings

Traders need to look at a lot of different data, but the first point you should look at is the company's earnings. This is the quickest way to find the best answer to the most common investing question. "How much money is the company making, and how much is it likely to make in the future?"

Basically, earnings are profits. This might be difficult to figure out, but that's what buying stocks of a company are all about. The good news is that companies will release their earnings every quarter. Analysts will make sure that they look at these reports over thoroughly, especially when dealing with major companies. When a company says their earnings are on the up, this will typically lead to a higher price in their stocks. Sometimes, this could also translate to a larger dividend. If the earnings fall short of expectations, the market can hammer it.

While earnings are important on their own, they don't tell you much. They don't look at how the market has the stocks valued. You will have to use fundamental analysis tools to get the full picture of the actual value of the stock. Most of the ratios can be figured out for you using finance sites, but they are also pretty easy to do on your own.

EPS, or earnings per share – The numbers of shares and the earnings can't tell you all that much about a company when looked at separately, but when combined, you will figure out the most commonly used ratios when it comes to analysis. EPS will show you the amount of the company's profit that belongs to every stock. You can figure this out by dividing the net income by the number of shares.

P/E, or price-to-earnings ratio – This will compare the sales price right now to the per-share earnings.

PEG, or projected earnings growth – PEG will provide you an estimate of the one-year earnings growth rate.

P/S, or price-to-sales – This will look at how the stock price compares to the revenue of the company. This may sometimes be seen as revenue multiple.

P/B, or price-to-book – This will compare the stock's book value with what the market value is. This can figure out by dividing the closing price by the book value from the last quarter.

Dividend payout ratio – This will compare dividends paid out to the stockholders to the total income. It also takes into account the retained earnings, which is income that will never be paid out but is kept for growth.

Dividend yield – This will provide you a yearly ratio of the dividends when compared to the share price. You will get this number as a percentage. To figure this out, you will divide the dividend payment of every share in one year with the value of the share.

Return on equity – All you need to do is divide the net income of the equity to figure out the return on equity.

Intrinsic Value

The main assumption of fundamental analysis is that it won't provide you with an accurate reflection of the company's value supported by the public data. The second assumption is that the value that is found through the company's data is more likely to be more related to the actual value of the stock.

This hypothetical value is what analysts will call intrinsic value. However, it is important to understand that this phrase means something very different to the stock would then it does when used in different contexts, like options.

The third assumption is that, in the long run, you will start seeing the market reflect the fundamentals. The main issue of this assumption is nobody knows how long this is going to take—this what fundamental analysis is all about. When you turn your attention to one business, a trader can estimate the intrinsic value and find opportunities to buy at a discount.

Criticisms of Fundamental Analysis

The biggest issues people have with this form of analysis can be divided into believers of the market hypothesis and technical analysis proponents.

Efficient Market Hypothesis
Those who fall into this category normally disagree about technical and fundamental analysis.
This hypothesis argues that it's impossible to beat the market through fundamental or technical analysis. Since the prices of all stocks on the market are at a chance for returns, then the market's is always unpredictable. This makes it nearly impossible for a person to outperform the market.

Technical Analysis
This is another form of analysis. Basically, people who perform this type of analysis will base all of their investments totally on the volume and price of the stocks. They will use charts and many other tools and they will trade based on the momentum while not looking at the fundamentals. A basic rule of technical analysis is that the market discounts everything. All of the news about a specific company will already be figure into the stock. This means that that the price movement is going to show you a lot more information than the fundamentals of business.

Chapter 6: Technical Analysis

The second type of analysis traders should understand technical analysis. This form of analysis will look at historical market data, which includes value and price. Technical analysts use quantitative analysis, behavioral economics, and market psychology to figure out how it performed in the past and how it could perform in the future. There are two forms of technical analysis; statistical indicators and chart patterns.

Technical analysis is basically a blanket term for several strategies that all depend on how a person interprets the price action. Most of the time, it is focused on figuring out if a current trend will continue or not. Some analysts swear by trendlines, while others prefer candlestick formations. The best analysis will use a combination of all of these tools to spot entry and exit points for trades. A formation of a chart could show you where to enter for a short sell, but it is best if a trader looks at the moving averages for various periods to make sure that it is likely to happen that way.

The basic principle of technical analysis is that the market price will reflect all available information that may affect the market. This means you do not need to look over the fundamental, new, or economic developments because they will already have been figured into the price. These analysts believe that a price will move in trends and that history will always repeat whenever you look over the psychology of the market.

The chart patterns are all subjective and are up to you to analyze and interpret the areas of resistance and support by looking for certain patterns. All of these patterns are made to help predict where the prices are headed, following a breakdown or breakout from a certain time and price point.

Technical indicators are a statistical type of analysis where you use math to help figure out the volume and price. You will most commonly see moving averages, which will smooth out the price data so that you can spot trends more easily. There are also complex indicators out there that will look at the interplay of several moving averages. There are a lot of trading systems that use a basis of technical indicators since they are all quantitatively figured.

Limitations

Technical analysis will have the same limitations of any strategy based on trade triggers. A person could misinterpret the chart. A chart formation may predict low volume. The time they used to mark the moving averages may have been marked too short or too long for the trade you are looking at. If you push those to the side, technical analysis has some fascinating limitations that are unique to just this type of analysis. As more of these techniques, tools, and strategies for technical analysis have been adopted, they will impact the movement of the price.

Analysis of Terminology

There are a lot of strange terms that you may not have heard or heard in passing, which is important if you want to understand what we will talk about in the rest of this chapter. Before we look at a couple of chart types of technical analysis, let's go over some terms you will need to understand.

Long

The simplest way to explain the word long is that it means to buy. When you are "going long" on the stock market, it just means that you are going to buy it. If you are already long, then you already own the stock. In the trading world, a person goes long if they believe that the item's price will go up. This way, you will have the chance to sell the stock for a higher price than what they had paid for it.

For example, Billy goes long on 100 shares of XYZ at $10, which costs him a total of $1,000. A few hours later, he sells those for $10.40 and collects $1040, making a profit of $40. Let's say the price falls to $9.50; this means that the position is no longer profitable. He would lose $50 if he were to sell at that point.

Bullish

When you are long, you are taking a bullish action. Simple, being a bull is caused by the belief that an asset is going to go up in value. Being a bull could represent an action or opinion. For a person to be considered bullish, they would have to go long on any assets that they want to remain bullish on. On the other hand, they could just have the opinion that the price is going to go up but choose not to make any trades because of their opinion. Having a bullish stance could just be a certain opinion about one stock or a broad opinion about the market overall.

Bullish gets its name from a bull, who strikes up with its horns causing the prices to go higher. A bull market happens when there is an uptrend as the prices rise, typically over a certain period, like years or months.

Short

A lot of people think trading is all about buying low and selling high, but that's not the only thing. Traders can choose to sell a stock at a high price and then buy it back once the price is lower. Being short basically means that when you are the first to sell, you hope that you can buy it back later on at a lesser price. Essentially, you borrow a stock, sell it, and then buy it again at a lesser price to make a profit on it later. If you do this, then you are short the asset. This can also be calling shorting or short-selling.

With the forex and futures market, you have the option to short whenever you want. With the stock market, you have restrictions on when you can short a stock. No matter which market you are using, if you hear that somebody is shorting something, they think the price is going to fall.

Let's look at Billy again with his 100 shares of XYZ that he shorts at $10. He sold first and made $1000, but the account reflects a negative 100 shares. You have to make sure that you change that negative back to zero at some time, and you do this by buying those shares back. After an hour, he purchases 100 shares at $9.60 for $960; this gives him a profit of $40. However, if the price ended up going up and not down, to say $10.50, he would lose $50.

Bear

Bearish is the opposite of being bullish. The person believes that the price is going to fall. A person could have a bearish belief about a company, or they could have a belief about an entire area. These may or may not act on their bearish beliefs. If they decide that they are going to act, they could sell any shares they have, or they may go short.

The bear's imagery is that it strikes down with its paws, which will make the prices go lower.

A bear market is a market that is currently in a downtrend that normally lasts over a certain period, like months or years.

Bar Chart

Bar charts are one form of technical analysis. Over time, it will show several price bars. Every bar lets you see how the prices have moved during a certain period. A daily chart lets you see the prices for every day. Every bar will normally show the open, high, low, and closing prices. You can also adjust the numbers that it shows. The study of these charts can help aid in making trading decisions. Bar charts give traders the chance to spot potential trend reversals, monitor price movement, and volatility, and analyze trends.

Each bar on the chart will have vertical lines that show the lowest and highest price reached during a certain period. You will find the opening price by looking for a tiny horizontal line on the main vertical line's left side. You will find the closing on the opposite side of the vertical. If the price closed at a higher price than it opened at, the bar would likely be colored green or black. However, if the opposite is true, then it will be red. The color coding aspect of the bars helps people see the changes in price more easily. Most charting platforms will allow you to color code charts.

The trader will also have the ability to pick the period they would like to analyze. You can pick a minute bare, which will be updated with every passing minute with a brand new bar. This would work for a day trader, but it wouldn't be that great for a long-term investor. A weekly chart will give a new bar every week and could be a better chart for the long-term investor, but it's not going to give enough information for a day trader.

Due to the numbers that the bar chart shows you, you can glean a lot of information from the chart. When you see a long vertical bar, it lets you know that there was a huge price change between the low and the high. This means that there was an increase in volatility during that time. If the chart had a small vertical bar, then there wasn't a lot of volatility.

If you notice a big difference between the close and open price, then the were some major price movements. If the closing and opening price were far apart, there was a lot of buying going on during that time, which could mean that more buying may occur. If they were close together, it means there wasn't a lot of conviction in price movement at this time.

Where the close is located in relation to the low and high can also tell you a lot. If the stock rallied more at this time, but the close still ended up being below the day's high, that means there were a lot of sellers close to the end of the periods. This is less bullish than if it closed near the high.

If you have a color-coded bar chart to show the rise or fall during the time, the colors will show you what you are looking for at a glance. An overall uptrend is normally shown using black or green bars, and it will have a strong uptrend in price movements. You will then see downtrends as red bars and strong down movement.

Bar charts would be a lot like the Japanese candlestick charts. They both will give you the same type of information, but it will just be in a different format. The bar chart has vertical lines with horizontal checks to show close and open. Candlestick charts will have vertical lines that show the high and low, called the wick or shadow, but the main difference between the close and open is depicted through a thicker area known as the real body. We'll get more into candlestick charts in just a moment.

Candlestick Charts

The candlestick chart was started over 100 years before the point-and-figure and bar charts. During the 1700s, Homma, a Japanese man, started noticing that, while supply and demand did affect the price of rice, there was also a huge influence by the emotions of the traders. Candlesticks show you the emotion through a visual representation of how the price moved along with different colors. These charts can be used to help a person make their trading decisions based on the patterns that occur regularly that will help to predict a short-term change in price.

On the candlestick, you will find all of the same numbers as shown on the bar chart. The widest part is known as the real body. This real body is what will show you the difference between the close and open of the day. If you see that it is colored in, then the close-ended up being lower than the opening cost had been.

If the real body is not colored in, then the stock closed at a higher cost than what it opened.

Right on top and just below this real body is the wicks or shadows. These are what show you the low and high prices of the day. If you see that the upper shadow is short, it is telling you that the open for the day was very close to what the high was. When you have a short upper on an up day, then the close was very close to the high. The close, high, low, and open relationship is going to determine how all of the candlesticks will look. You can see a real body that is short or long and white or black, and the wicks may be short or long. The candlestick chart is more visual because of the color coding and the thicker real bodies, which can help you see the close and open differences.

A candlestick will get formed with the various movement of a stock's price. While the price movement can look random at times, there are other times when you will start to see a pattern, which can help you make trading decisions. There are a lot of patterns you can get with a candlestick chart, and we'll go over some now.

These patterns can then be further separated between bullish and bearish. When prices are probably going to go up, then it is bullish. If the prices are likely to go down, then it is bearish. There is no one pattern that is going to work every single time, as these patterns will only should your tendencies and not a guarantee.

The bearish engulfing pattern is one pattern you should keep a lookout for. This will happen when there is an uptrend when the buyers outnumber the number of sellers. This action can be seen through a long, red body that is engulfed by a short, green body. This lets you know that the sellers are once again in control and that there Is a good chance that the price is going to go down.

Then you have the bullish engulfing pattern. This is the opposite of the other, and means that the number of buyers outweigh the sellers. The is shown when there is a long green body that engulfs a short red body. When bulls have gained control, the prices will likely go up.

Another pattern is the bearish evening star. The pattern is topped by a star. You can figure this one out by looking for the last candle in the pattern and if it opened under the previous day's small body. This body could be green or red. The last candle of the series is going to close deep in the body of the candle of two days before. This will tell you that there is a stall with the buyers and the sellers are gaining control. There could be more selling to come.

A bearish harami pattern can be found when there is a small red body that is fully inside the body from the previous day. This isn't really a pattern to act on, but it is one that you may want to keep an eye on. The pattern tells you that there is some sort of indecision when it comes to the buyers. If this prices goes up more, it could be indicating that there is an uptrend, but if there is another down candle, this indicates a further slide. Like with the other two we have talked about, you have the opposite of the bearish harami, which is the bullish harami. This one will let you know that if you get another up day, then there could be an uptrend occurring.

Remember that these are only a few different patterns that you can find on a candlestick chart. Also, they are not guarantees. You can't count on these patterns alone to tell you whether or not you should buy or sell a stock. You need to take several other things into consideration to make the best decision possible. There are no guarantees in the stock market. Thinking something is a guarantee is the quickest way to lose your money, so always make the smart decision to research a trade before you make it.

Chapter 7: Guiding Principles

Being a swing trader isn't something you should do just for fun. You have to make sure you know what you're doing and treat it as such. This is why it is important to follow some basic guiding principles. The number one thing you want to make sure you do is to treat your swing trading like you would treat your own business.

Trading needs to be looked at with the same discipline you would have as a business. Coming up with a written trading plan is an important first step, which we will discuss in a moment. You should also come up with your own accounting system to track your trading results and keep up with your brokerage reports. A simple excel spreadsheet with monthly, daily, and weekly results is all you need. You should make sure you include equity, net profit or loss, ECN costs, commission costs, number of trades, gross profit or loss, and any other data that you find helpful. This data can be used to improve your trading. You can look at patterns and find profit and cost relationships.

For example, you could see that you have gained three days in a row and then lose for two. If this continues to repeat, you can correct your work to reach more consistent results and have a more effective risk management plan. You might notice that you trade better during the morning and then give back some of your profits in the afternoon. This could mean that you need to stop trading during the afternoon for a bit or implement tighter controls for the session. When it comes to profit/cost relationships, let's assume that you have noticed costs as a percentage of the gross profit is typically about 30% but has been slowly rising. This could show that you have been overtrading and that you need to slow down.

You also need to make sure that you have a good filing system. You should keep your daily printouts from your platform. This shows you all of the trades that you made that day, and you can match it to your brokerage reports. Mistakes can occur, even when you are using advanced software. You are the only person that will keep a good eye on your money.

Coming up with a trading diary is a good idea. You should make sure that you include comments about what you did right and what didn't work. Did you follow through on your rules and plan? What changes do you need to make so that you don't make the same mistakes? If your strategy working the way, it's supposed to? Do you need to change your share size? You may find that you need to change your risk management parameters. These are the questions you need to go over. Having a trading diary is a great way to keep track of your progress and acknowledge the things you have done well.

Capital Preservation

You need to have your trading plan and rules designed to preserve your capital and avoid any huge losses that could empty out your trading account. If you end up losing all of your trading capital, you won't be able to make any more trades. To preserve your money, you will have to use a combination of risk management and money management. Your main responsibility is not to lose your money and not make a lot of money as fast as possible.

You have to know how to control your risk and to keep any losses you make small. If you need a refresher on how to do that, refer back to the risk management chapter. I can't overemphasize this enough. You may start out by saying, "This is obvious," but there are very few new traders, a lot of experienced traders, or don't take the time to come up with a risk management place. Quit trying to find the secret to high-profit trading and turn your attention to controlling risk.

Having a money management strategy will help to figure out how much you should trade. For example, if your account is at $25,000, should you enter a trade that uses all of your capital? That's not your best course of action. If you did that, and the trade went sideways, you might end up taking too big of a loss with that one trade. Pick out a dollar amount or percentage of your total that is the max you are willing to use on a single trade. This is going to control your losses.

take a gamble on their money. Anytime you trade in front of a report is always thought of as a gamble since you can't know how the markets are going to react.

6. Trade Preparations

Whatever program and system you use for trading, label the minor and major support and resistance levels, come up with alerts for exit and entry, and make sure that you can easily see all of the signals with a clear auditory or visual signal.

7. Create Some Exit Rules

A lot of traders will mistakenly focus all their time on finding "buy signals," but they won't pay attention to where to buy and when to get out. Most traders can't sell a stock if it is down since they don't want to take a loss. You have to deal with it and learn how to accept your losses, or you aren't going to make it as a trader. If you hit a stop, then you were wrong. It's nothing personal. Ask any professional trader, and they will tell you that they have lost more trades than they have ever worn, but they still end up making profits by managing their money and limiting their losses.

Before you get into any trade, you have to know where you should exit. There will always be two probably exits for every trade. Do you first need to figure out your stop-loss order? This has to be written down. A mental stop is not going to work. Second, every trade needs to have a profit-target. Once you have reached that point, sell part of what you have, and then you can switch up your stop-loss to the breakeven point.

8. Set Entry Rules

This is after exits because exits are more important. You want to make sure that your system is complicated enough that it is effective but simple so that it will help with a snap decision. If you were to come up with 20 conditions that you have to meet and most of them are subjective, you are going to find it pretty hard, possibly impossible, to make any sort of trade. In fact, computers are often a lot better at this than a person, which is the reason why computers do almost 50 percent of the trades happening on the NYSE

There are no feelings or thinking when it comes to computers. If the conditions get met, then they enter. If things go sideways or the profit-target gets reached, then they exit. They don't get upset or feel invincible. Every decision is based upon odds and not emotions.

9. Keep Excellent Records

The majority of successful traders are also really good at keeping up with their records. If they win, they are going to know what they did right and how. What's most important is that they want to know the same information even if they lose. That's to ensure they don't make the same mistakes. You need to write down the details like entry and exit, targets, the time, support and resistance, daily opening range, market open and close, and write down comments about the reasons why you made the trade and anything you learned about it.

You need to save your records to make sure that you will be able to analyze what you made and what you lost with certain systems, drawdowns, average time per trade, and other important information. It would be best if you also compared these things to your strategy. You are running a business, and you are also working as its accountant. You are going to want the business to be successful and profitable.

10. Analyze Performance

At the close of every day, figuring up what you made or lost should be secondary to the reasons why you did that and how. Write out all of your conclusions so that you can look back on them. There are always going to be losing trades. The important thing is that you make sure you have a plan that is going to allow you to win over the long term.

Chapter 8: Rules

Being a swing trader can be exhilarating work, and it definitely isn't for everybody. The action is fast, so you have to be ready for everything. To make sure you are prepared, let's go over some simple rules about swing trading.

1. Cap Your Account

You can lose your money as quickly as you make it in swing trading. This is why you will need to start a separate account. This will keep you from being tempted to trade with more money than what you are going to be able to afford.

2. Look for Volatile Markets

To have the most successful trades, you will need to figure out which stocks are showing wide short-term fluctuations. You want things to be as wide as possible. If there is a narrow trading range, then the trade won't be able to generate the profit it needs.

3. Be Consistent

Come up with a plant, and then stick to it. Much like being a baseball player who has found himself in a slump and start to experiment with how they swing and their stance, which doesn't help, you are going to find it much more difficult to get back in if you try to experiment with the rules. The only place you should be experimenting in is your practice account or on paper, and never when you are putting real money on the line.

4. Know The Market Phases
You might not be trading on trends; you should be following the basic trends to get a better feel for your swings' duration and direction. If you have a bearish market, the upswings could be weaker than when it's bull.

5. Know Support and Resistance Levels
Resistance and support will define the trading range, whether things are going up, down, or flat. If you keep track of a stock's movement within this range, you will not have too much trouble with monitoring the swings. You will be able to spot a breakout or a fallout.

6. Know Your Entry and Exit
This is all a part of the plan that you came up with before you started trading. You have to know what will trigger your buy and sell orders.

7. Use Stop-Loss
You have to have these orders put in place to help protect your position. I've said this several times already, so just set your stop-loss orders.

8. Cut Your Losses
If the stock isn't performing the way you expected, then cut your losses quickly. This will help to free up your money so that you can make another trade.

9. Take your Profits

It can be extremely tempting to let your profits build up as much as possible, but the problem is, profits can disappear very fast. If the stock you bought is in a good upward swing, then take half of the profit when it gets close to the resistance level and ensure that the stop-loss is placed tightly behind the last position.

10. Don't Take Chances

Over the long run, you will make money if you make sure that you stick to your plan. You should not gamble. You should not take chances. You are going to have some losses, but when you win, it should be more than enough to compensate for what you lost. If you end up straying from your plan, then the odds you will win will be reduced.

Penny Stocks

One thing we have not talked about is penny stocks. They tend to be attractive to traders, especially the new ones because they are inexpensive. You can grab up a couple of thousands just for a hundred dollars or so. While you can swing trade penny stocks, it is typically not a good idea.

All types of trading or investing will come with some risk. Prices change, the world changes and things can happen, but with penny stocks, that risk becomes much higher. The world of penny stocks is filled with pumpers and manipulators who are looking to take advantage of traders, especially the new traders.

There are a lot of scammers and promoters out there in the penny stock world who wants you to buy their stock for some reason. Sometimes, because they have a lot of shares and they would love to sell them to you. Does this seem messed up? Well, that's because it is. However, you don't need to let all of this scare you off completely. You can trade penny stocks intelligently and safely. You can minimize the risk and lower your risk exposure by making sure that you know what you're doing.

You are going to have to have a special strategy to swing trade penny stocks. Penny stocks are any stocks under $5 and below, and that's according to the SEC. Since most of these will trade for pennies, they aren't found on the major exchanges. The major exchanges will de-list any stock that goes for under a dollar.

If you decide to take the risk of trading penny stocks, the first thing you need to do is your own research. Never, ever, take another person's work about a stock. Just because a person is promising or expecting a huge return does not mean that it will happen. If a story were to sound too good to be true, it likely is. Always look for a respectable trading company.

Also, you should always be on the lookout for pump and dumps. The penny stock sector often has more selling happening than buying. This is because some people get paid by companies to pump their stocks for them. While it is illegal, people do it anyway. They aren't making money by trading the stocks. Instead, they make money by getting paid to get you to make the trade. They simply get paid to advertise stocks.

You also have to pay attention to the charts when it comes to swing trading. Suppose somebody is saying that a stock or sector doesn't follow the charts, the turn away. This is especially true for those without proper stock training. The charts will confirm the pump and dumps. It would be best if you kept an eye on the head and shoulders patterns. This is what is known as the F you pattern, which is what will happen if you wind up getting caught at the end of its formation.

I would suggest avoiding swing trading penny stocks for anybody who has never traded before. It is too easy to fall into a trap if you don't know what to pay attention to. I know the prices are attractive, but it's better to avoid them than end up losing your money.

Chapter 9: Strategies

Swing trading is normally defined as a short-term trade that only lasts between one day and one month. Day traders normally try to capture a piece of a good move, while swing traders try to capture a whole leg or when it swings either up or down.

Swing trading has many forms; some will trade in classical chart patterns such as "head and shoulders" while others trade "the short-term sentiment reading," and others will take a more significant approach.

Below you will find five strategies that will be helpful in finding opportunities while managing your trades from beginning to end. You will use these techniques to any stock that you are want to find, probably entry points. You could use tools like a scanner that recognizes patterns, which can help you to find stocks.

Ten and 20-Day SMA

Another good technique will be involved using SMAs or "simple moving averages." These help to smooth out the data on prices by figuring out the average price that is constantly updated. These SMAs can be figured out for a certain period or number of days. Let's say you had a ten-day SMA that gives you the daily closing prices for the past ten days. Then you would divide it by ten to get the average for each day.

Every average will be connected to the following so that you will have a single smooth line that can help get rid of the "noise" on the stock charts. The length can be used for any interval on a chart, from something as short as a minute to up to a week. An SMA that has a short length will react faster to the price changes than the ones with a longer time frame. With the ten and 20-day SMA system, you will apply two SMAs that are either ten or 20-days in length on your chart. Once the tend-day reaches the 20-day SMA, you will get a buy signal. This shows you that an uptrend has started. If the shorter SMA crosses under, the longer one, you will get a sell signal because this kind of SMA shows a downtrend.

Channel Trading

For this strategy, you will have to find a stock that is showing a strong trend and is trading within a specific channel. If you have a channel that has already been plotted around a bearish trend, you will want to think about opening up a sell if the price were to bound down from that top line. If you use these channels to trade, you must trade during trends. That means if you notice that a price is going down, then you will need to find a position to sell as long as the price breaks from the channel, move higher, and then reveals a reversal. This will become a new uptrend.

Resistance and Support Triggers

Resistance and support lines are the cornerstone of technical analysis. This is where you can come up with a great swing trading strategy.

Support levels show an area or price level on a chart underneath the current market price where the buyer would have the strength to overcome the pressure of selling. Because of this, a price decline gets stopped, and the price goes back up again. The trader will want to enter the trade once the price bounces from the support. You would place your stop-loss right under this line.

Resistance, as we could figure out by the name, is the opposite to support. It shows an area or price level over the market price where the pressure to sell overcomes the pressure to buy. This can cause the price to lower. This is when the trader needs to enter a trade when the price bounces off the resistance. You would then place your stop-loss right above this line. The main thing to keep in mind when you use resistance and support in your system is that anytime a price breaches a certain level, it switches roles. Basically, what used to be supported will become resistance, etc.

Fibonacci Retracement

This pattern could help swing traders find resistance and support levels, which makes it possible for reversals on the charts. Stocks will usually retrace a certain amount in a trend before they get reversed. Horizontal lines can be marked at the Fibonacci ratios of 61.8, 23.6, and 38.2 on a chart to show reversals. Traders typically look at around the 50 percent spot as well, even though it doesn't actually fit into Fibonacci since most stocks will reverse after tracing the moves they already made.

You can apply or all of the strategies we have discussed into your system to help you spot the best opportunities to trade the markets you would like to trade-in. Most advance charts on your different trading platforms tend to come equipped with these various indicators listed above, along with the tools you need to put these strategies into play.

Chapter 10: Entry and Exit

This chapter will discuss entry and exit strategies to help you know when to buy and sell your stocks.

Entry Strategy

What is likely the most important part of any trade is your entry strategy. This when you are placing your capital at risk since you are putting it into a trade. When the stock does move in your favor, you will be able to relax, manage your stocks, and then wait for a graceful exit.

This chapter is going to take the time to explain the basic price patterns that are most often used when it comes to entering. When you have a better idea of these things, you can start to try out advanced strategies based on certain patterns that you might be trading. When it comes to any entry strategy, the first thing you are going to want to do is to find your swing points. A swing point is a pattern that contains three candles. If you are entering a long position, you will need to find a low swing point. If you are entering a short position, you will need to find a high swing point.

Finding Reversals By Using Swing Points
If you are looking for a low swing point:

- One candle means that it is low

- A second candle means that it is a lower low
- When you find a third, it makes it a higher low

A third candle lets you know that the sellers have become weak and that the stock is more likely going to reverse.

If you are looking for a high swing point:

- Finding a candle make it a high
- A second candle means that you have a higher high
- A third candle means that you have a lower high

This third candle lets you know that the buyers have become weak and that there is a good chance that there is going to be a reversal.

When it comes to a long entry strategy, you are going to want to find the stocks that have pulled back and have started to create a low swing point.

Please note that not every swing point will bring about a powerful reversal. The reversal isn't going to work without having swing points. Take the time to look through some stock charts and look at the reversals that have happened to spot the patterns more quickly.

Consecutive Price Patterns
It is ideal that you will trade stocks that have several down days before developing a swing point. This is

your best-case scenario. The complete opposite happens on the short side. When it comes to that scenario, you will look for days that have been consecutively up before the high swing point develops. If you want to develop swing points, you will need to look at the chart's left-hand side to see if it has a resistance or support area on the chart. This is going to help with the reliability of the stock and the entry strategy.

Now that you know how to get into a trade let's take a look at the best way to get out.

Exit Strategies

"Traders will spend countless hours fine-tuning their entry strategies, but they blow their accounts by taking a bad exit. Most traders don't have good exit planning, and they often get shaken out at the worst price. You can fix this with some basic strategies that can help your profits. Before we get into the strategies, we will begin looking at why the holding period is so important. Then we can move onto the concept of market timing that is so misunderstood. Last we will cover the stop and scaling methods that can reduce your losses and protect your profits.

Holding Periods
It is completely impossible to talk about exit strategies without seeing how important a holding period works with your strategy when trading. These time frames

will line up with the broad approach that will take money out of the markets:

- Investment timing: Weeks or months
- Position Trading: Days or weeks
- Swing Trading: Hours or days
- Day Trading: Minutes or hours

Choose a category that will line up the closest with your market approach because this can dictate just how long you have to get a loss of profit. Stick with your parameters, or you might risk moving a trade into an investment or turning a momentum play into a scalp. This type of approach will take some discipline since some positions do better, and you decide to keep them longer than you should. Even though you can squeeze and stretch your holding period to consider all the market conditions and then take your exit within the parameters will build your trading skills, profits, and confidence.

Market Timing
You need to get into a habit of establishing your risk and reward targets before you enter into a trade. You need to look at all the charts and find the next resistance level that will come into play inside the time constraints in your holding period. This will mark your target reward. You will then have to find the price where you can be proven wrong if the security changes and hits it. This is your risk target. Now you have to calculate your reward to risk ratio and look for a two to one in your favor. If you go with

anything less than this, you need just to skip this trade and find a better opportunity.

Try to focus on managing your trades on two key prices. Let's say that things are going your way, and the price is moving toward your target reward. The price's rate of change will now come into play since the faster it can get to your magic number, then you will have more flexibility when picking a favorable exit. The first option you have would e to take a blind exit when it gets to the price you want. You can pat yourself on the back for a great job and then move on to your next trade. Another better option would be when the price is strongly trending in your favor, just let it go past the reward target and then place a protective stop when the price is at a certain level while you are attempting to add some gains. Now you can look for the next barrier, which is remaining positioned for as long as you can if it doesn't violate the time you can hold your stock.

Slow advances can be trickier to trade since most securities will get close but won't reach your reward target. This means you are going to need a profit protection strategy that will kick into gear when the price has gone about 75 percent of the distance between your reward and risk targets. You will need to put a trailing stop that will protect any partial gains. If you are doing real-time trading, keep a finger on the exit button while you are watching the ticker tape. The trick is to remain positioned until the price's action gives you a good reason to get out.

If the position goes better than expected, it might gap above your reward target. You can respond with a protective stop when it reaches the reward target. You can raise it each night if the upside makes more progress.

Stop Loss Strategies
Stops have to go where they can get you out if security violates the reason you took the trade. This can be confusing for traders who were taught to put stops based on values such as a five percent drawdown or $1.50 less than the price it was at entry. These placements might not make any sense since they haven't been tuned into that tool's volatility and characteristics. Rather, you should use certain technical features such as moving averages, round numbers, and trendlines to figure out the natural "stop-loss price."

Modern markets require one more step to create an effective stop placement. Algorithms can target normal stop-loss levels, shake out the players, and then jump across resistance or support. This means that the stops have to be placed away from numbers that say you are wrong, and you should get out. Finding the right price to stay away from the stop runs is more of an art form than a science. The general rule is if you are in a low volatility trade, an addition of ten to 15 cents will work. If you are in a momentum play, it will require 50 to 75 cents more. You have a lot more options if you are watching in real-time since you can get out at your original target. Then you can reenter if the price goes back across the contested level."

Chapter 11: Creating a Routine

Swing trading combines technical and fundamental analysis to catch movements in prices while staying away from times that the market is idle. There are some benefits to this kind of trading. You are going to have more efficient use of your money while also getting bigger returns. The main drawbacks would be more volatility and larger commissions.

Swing trading could be a challenge for a normal trader. Professional traders will have lower commissions, information, leverage, and experience. Still, they are mostly limited by the tools, a larger capital, and risk that they can take. Most larger companies tend to trade in sizes that are much too large to move stocks in and out of quickly.

Retail traders that are known could take advantage of all these things to have a consistent profit. Here are what a good swing trader's strategy and routine could look like and the best ways to be successful when it comes to trading.

Pre-Market

Swing traders usually start their day around six o'clock in the morning EST. This is a long time before the opening bell rings for the day. This time is critical for getting a feel for the market on any given day, finding possible trades, making their daily watchlist, and checking on their existing positions.

Market Overview
The first thing they are going to do is check the news to see if there have been any new developments with the markets. The easiest way to do this is by watching CNBC or websites like Market Watch. All traders have to watch three things:

- Current holdings like SEC filings, earnings, news, etc.
- Sector sentiments like growing sectors, hot sectors, etc.
- The market's overall sentiment like overseas trading sessions, currency, inflation, key economic reports, bearish and bullish

Finding Possible Trades
Now, they have to check to see what trades they will make that day. Normally, they are going to enter a position using a fundamental catalyst and exit or manage a position through technical analysis. There are a couple of different ways to look for these fundamental catalysts

- Sector Plays

These can be found by looking at reputable financial websites or watching the news to figure out which sectors are doing well. If a trader wants a higher risk to get higher returns, they might decide to look for more obscure sectors like titanium or coal. These are usually harder to analyze, but they might yield a larger return. This kind of play makes the swing trader have to buy into trends at just the right time and ride these trends until they find retracement or reversal signs. Chart breaks are another kind of opportunity that is available to swing traders. These are normally stocks that get heavily traded that are close to a resistance level or key support. Swing traders have to look at several different types of patterns that were made to predict breakdowns and breakouts like Gann levels, Fibonacci levels, Wolfe Waves, channels, triangles, and many others.

Notice that the chart breaks can only be significant if a stock has plenty of interest. This will involve the trader buying after a breakout has occurred and the selling happening shortly after another resistance level shows up.

- Special Opportunities

You can find these things through SEC filings and sometimes in headlines on the news. These changes might include acquisitions, restructurings, mergers, takeovers, buyouts, insider buying, bankruptcies, initial public offerings, and other events. Normally, these can be found by looking at specific SEC filings like 13D and S-4. You can do this by using some sites like SECFiliings.com that sends notifications when the filings have been made. These opportunities usually carry a certain amount of risk, but they will provide you with different types of rewards if you can carefully look through all of the opportunities. These kinds of plays mean the swing traders have to buy when most people are selling and then selling when everybody else decides to buy. This tries to "fade" the overreactions that the news tends to spread.

Making a Watch List
The next thing you are going to want to come up with is a watch list of stocks that you may want to trade during the day. You will want to make sure that they have fundamental catalysts and have a good shot at being a good trade.

Check Your Existing Positions
During the hours before the market opens, you will need to look at all of the positions you have and ensure that nothing has come up within the market overnight that could derail you. This can easily be done by searching the stock symbol in a search engine like Google News.

The next thing that a trader will check is to see if any filings have been made by looking at the SEC's EDGAR database. If there is some information, you need to analyze it so you can figure out if it will affect your current trading plan. Traders could have to adjust their stop-loss and other orders because of this.

Market Hours
"Normal market hours are from 9:30 AM until 4 PM EST. It is within these hours that you will be watching and making trades. Most swing traders will look at "level II quotes," which shows who is selling and

buying and what amounts they are making their trades.

People entering swing trading that are used to be day traders will usually check on what market maker is making trades. This can be a cue for traders that tell them who is making all the trades. It helps them be more aware of fake bids and asks that they have been placed just to confuse traders.

Once you have found a viable trade, you will enter it and then start looking for a way to exit. This is usually done by using some kind of technical analysis. Most swing traders will use Fibonacci extensions, price by volume, or simple resistance levels. This needs to be done before the trade has been placed, but many things depend on trading for the day. Adjustments might have to be made later on, and this all depends on the trading's future.

One general rule you should follow is you shouldn't adjust your position and take on more of a risk. You should only adjust the profit-taking levels if the trading continues looking bullish, or you need to adjust a stop-loss level to make it go upward to make more of a profit.

Entering trades is usually more of an art form than a science, and it will depend on the activity during the day's trading. Managing your trades and exiting needs always to be an exact science.

The Market After Hours

Trading after the market closes isn't usually the time to do any swing trading since the market is illiquid, as the spread is just too vast. The most important aspect of after-hours trading are evaluating your stocks' performance. You need to write down all your trades carefully and any ideas you got for evaluation and tax purposes.

It is important to evaluate your stock's performance. In order to do this, you need to look at all the trading activity and find the things that need to be improved. Last but certainly not least, traders have to review their opening positions another time and pay attention to all the earnings announcements that come in after the market closes. You also need to look at other events that might impact your holdings. So, basically, you need to adopt a daily routine for trading like the one above to help you improve your trading while ultimately beating the market returns. It just takes some proper planning, preparation, and good resources."

Conclusion

Thank you for making it through to the end of the book; let's hope it was informative and able to provide you with all of the tools you need to achieve your goals, whatever they may be.

The next step is to take a look at your situation and see if swing trading is something for you. Once you know you have the overhead you need to make a go of this, you can start coming up with your strategy. Figure out what you want to invest in. Do you want to focus on stocks, or do you want to try something different like currencies or ETFs? It's up to you and your risk management strategy. You never want to lose more than you can afford, so make sure you have a solid plan for when things go unexpectedly. Swing trading can be lucrative income, but you have to make sure you know what you're doing and are well prepared.

Finally, if you found this book useful in any way, a review on Amazon is always appreciated!

www.ingramcontent.com/pod-product-compliance
Lightning Source LLC
Chambersburg PA
CBHW070809220526
45466CB00002B/605